Thank you
For buying
This book

How to Draw
People

TONY R. SMITH

How to Draw

People

AUTHOR TONY R. SMITH

Copyright © 2019 by Tony R. Smith. All Rights Reserved.

No part of this publication may be reproduced, distributed, or transmitted in any form or by any means, including photocopying, recording, or other electronic or mechanical methods, or by any information storage and retrieval system without the prior written permission of Smith Show Publishing, except in the case of very brief quotations embodied in critical reviews and certain other noncommercial uses permitted by copyright law.

How to use this book. First look at the picture that has been provided. Next, you draw your version of the animal. There are over thirty different drawings for you to practice. Have fun!

Our drawing

Your drawing

FOLLOW THE STEPS
DRAW ON THE NEXT PAGE

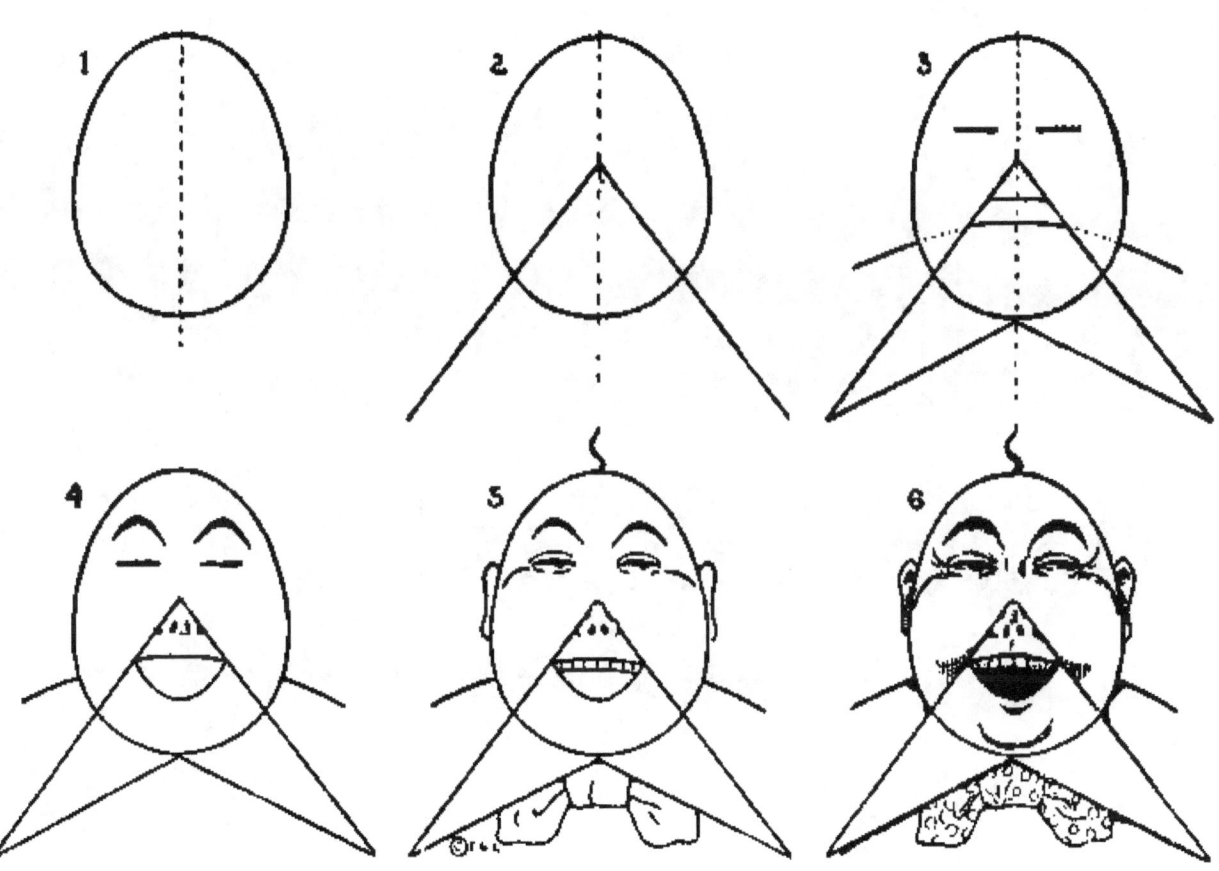

Bonus Sketch Paper

FOLLOW THE STEPS
DRAW ON THE NEXT PAGE

Bonus Sketch Page

DRAW THESE FACE ON THE NEXT PAGE

Bonus Sketch Page

DRAW THESE FACES ON THE NEXT PAGE

Bonus Sketch Page

Time to warm up.
Shade in the following
Shapes below.

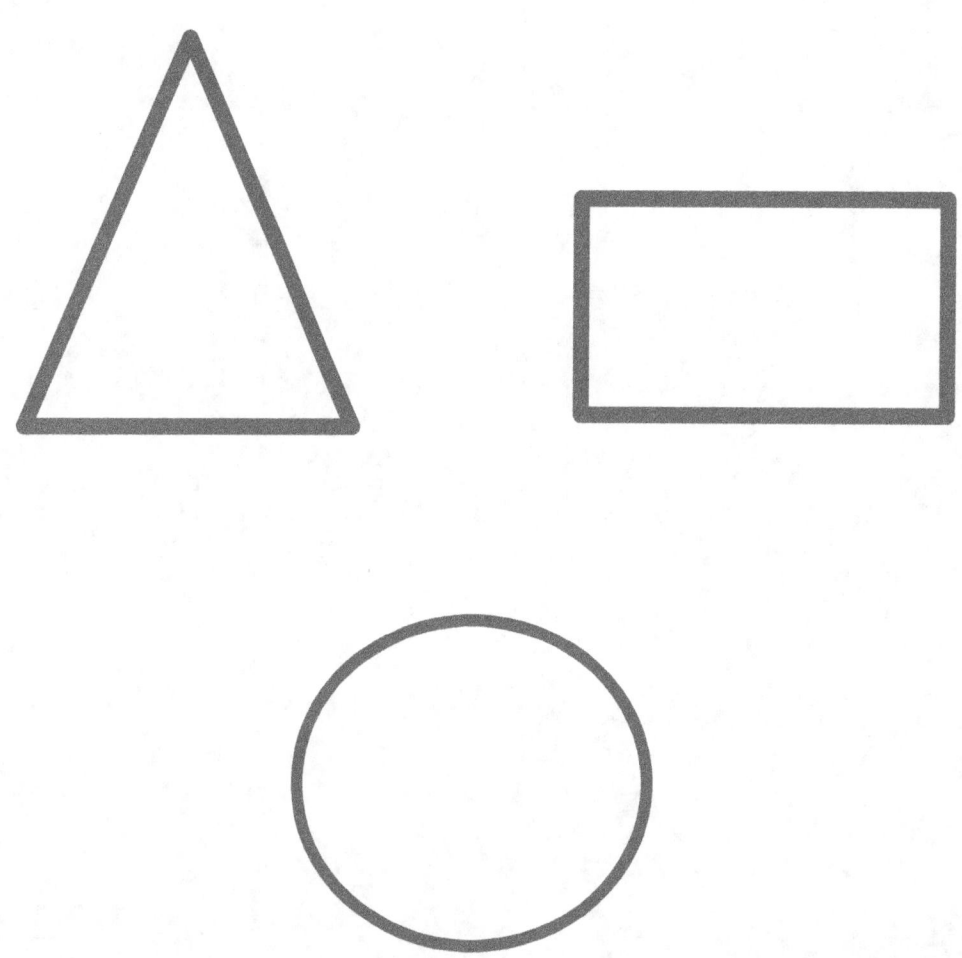

Bonus Sketch Paper

Bonus Sketch Page

Bonus Sketch Page

PRACTICE ON THIS PAGE. DRAW ON THE NEXT PAGE

Bonus Sketch Page

PRACTICE ON THIS PAGE.
DRAW ON THE NEXT PAGE

Bonus Sketch Page

PRACTICE ON THIS PAGE.
DRAW ON THE NEXT PAGE

Bonus Sketch Page

PRACTICE ON THIS PAGE.
DRAW ON THE NEXT PAGE

Bonus Sketch Page

PRACTICE ON THIS PAGE.
DRAW ON THE NEXT PAGE

Bonus Sketch Page

PRACTICE ON THIS PAGE.
DRAW ON THE NEXT PAGE

Bonus Sketch Page

PRACTICE ON THIS PAGE.
DRAW ON THE NEXT PAGE

Bonus Sketch Page

PRACTICE ON THIS PAGE. DRAW ON THE NEXT PAGE

Bonus Sketch Page

PRACTICE ON THIS PAGE.
DRAW ON THE NEXT PAGE

Bonus Sketch Page

PRACTICE ON THIS PAGE. DRAW ON THE NEXT PAGE

Bonus Sketch Page

PRACTICE ON THIS PAGE. DRAW ON THE NEXT PAGE

Bonus Sketch Page

PRACTICE ON THIS PAGE. DRAW ON THE NEXT PAGE

Bonus Sketch Page

PRACTICE ON THIS PAGE. DRAW ON THE NEXT PAGE

Bonus Sketch Page

PRACTICE ON THIS PAGE. DRAW ON THE NEXT PAGE

Bonus Sketch Page

PRACTICE ON THIS PAGE.
DRAW ON THE NEXT PAGE

Bonus Sketch Page

PRACTICE ON THIS PAGE.
DRAW ON THE NEXT PAGE

Bonus Sketch Page

PRACTICE ON THIS PAGE.
DRAW ON THE NEXT PAGE

Bonus Sketch Page

PRACTICE ON THIS PAGE. DRAW ON THE NEXT PAGE

Bonus Sketch Page

PRACTICE ON THIS PAGE.
DRAW ON THE NEXT PAGE

Bonus Sketch Page

PRACTICE ON THIS PAGE. DRAW ON THE NEXT PAGE

Bonus Sketch Page

PRACTICE ON THIS PAGE.
DRAW ON THE NEXT PAGE

Bonus Sketch Page

PRACTICE ON THIS PAGE.
DRAW ON THE NEXT PAGE

Bonus Sketch Page

PRACTICE ON THIS PAGE. DRAW ON THE NEXT PAGE

Bonus Sketch Page

PRACTICE ON THIS PAGE.
DRAW ON THE NEXT PAGE

Bonus Sketch Page

PRACTICE ON THIS PAGE. DRAW ON THE NEXT PAGE

Bonus Sketch Page

PRACTICE ON THIS PAGE. DRAW ON THE NEXT PAGE

Bonus Sketch Page

PRACTICE ON THIS PAGE.
DRAW ON THE NEXT PAGE

Bonus Sketch Page

PRACTICE ON THIS PAGE.
DRAW ON THE NEXT PAGE

Bonus Sketch Page

PRACTICE ON THIS PAGE. DRAW ON THE NEXT PAGE

Bonus Sketch Page

PRACTICE ON THIS PAGE. DRAW ON THE NEXT PAGE

Bonus Sketch Page

PRACTICE ON THIS PAGE. DRAW ON THE NEXT PAGE

Bonus Sketch Page

PRACTICE ON THIS PAGE.
DRAW ON THE NEXT PAGE

Bonus Sketch Page

PRACTICE ON THIS PAGE. DRAW ON THE NEXT PAGE

Bonus Sketch Page

PRACTICE ON THIS PAGE. DRAW ON THE NEXT PAGE

Bonus Sketch Page

PRACTICE ON THIS PAGE. DRAW ON THE NEXT PAGE

Bonus Sketch Page

PRACTICE ON THIS PAGE. DRAW ON THE NEXT PAGE

Bonus Sketch Page

PRACTICE ON THIS PAGE. DRAW ON THE NEXT PAGE

Bonus Sketch Page

PRACTICE ON THIS PAGE. DRAW ON THE NEXT PAGE

Bonus Sketch Page

PRACTICE ON THIS PAGE. DRAW ON THE NEXT PAGE

Bonus Sketch Page

PRACTICE ON THIS PAGE. DRAW ON THE NEXT PAGE

Bonus Sketch Page

PRACTICE ON THIS PAGE. DRAW ON THE NEXT PAGE

Bonus Sketch Page

PRACTICE ON THIS PAGE. DRAW ON THE NEXT PAGE

Bonus Sketch Page

PRACTICE ON THIS PAGE. DRAW ON THE NEXT PAGE

Bonus Sketch Page

PRACTICE ON THIS PAGE.
DRAW ON THE NEXT PAGE

Bonus Sketch Page

PRACTICE ON THIS PAGE.
DRAW ON THE NEXT PAGE

Bonus Sketch Page

PRACTICE ON THIS PAGE.
DRAW ON THE NEXT PAGE

Bonus Sketch Page

PRACTICE ON THIS PAGE.
DRAW ON THE NEXT PAGE

Bonus Sketch Page

PRACTICE ON THIS PAGE. DRAW ON THE NEXT PAGE

Bonus Sketch Page

Bonus Sketch Page

Bonus Sketch Page

Copyright 2019, S.S. Publishing/All Right Reserved
No part of this publication may be reproduced in whole or in part, shared with others, stored in a retrieval system, digitized or transmitted in any form without written permission from the publisher.

www.ingramcontent.com/pod-product-compliance
Lightning Source LLC
Chambersburg PA
CBHW081725100526
44591CB00016B/2500